Communicating effectively with people with a learning disability

Sue Thurman

Supporting the level 2 and 3 Diplomas in
Health and Social Care (learning disability pathway)
and the Common Induction Standards

all about people

Acknowledgements

Photographs from www.crocodilehouse.co.uk and James Cooper. Our thanks to Lottie, Sophie and Edward and to Choices Housing and Elizabeth Fitzroy for their help and support.

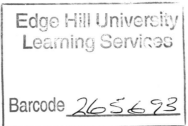
First published in 2011 jointly by Learning Matters Ltd and the British Institute of Learning Disabilities

British Library Cataloguing in Publication Data
A CIP record for this book is available from the British Library

ISBN: 978 0 85725 510 5

Ths book is also available in the following ebook formats:
Adobe ebook ISBN: 978 0 85725 512 9
EPUB ebook ISBN: 978 0 85725 511 2
Kindle ISBN: 978 0 85725 513 6

Cover design by Pentacor
Text design by Pentacor
Project Management by Deer Park Productions, Tavistock
Typeset by Pantek Arts Ltd, Maidstone
Printed and bound in Great Britain by Ashford Colour Press Ltd, Gosport, Hants

Learning Matters Ltd
20 Cathedral Yard
Exeter
EX1 1HB
Tel: 01392 215560
E-mail: info@learningmatters.co.uk
www.learningmatters.co.uk

BILD
Campion House
Green Street
Kidderminster
Worcestershire
DY10 1JL
Tel: 01562 723010
E-mail: enquiries@bild.org.uk
www.bild.org.uk

Contents

This book covers:

- Common Induction Standards – Standard 3 – Communicate effectively
- Level 2 and Level 3 diploma units SHC 21 – Introduction to communication in health, social care or children's and young people's settings and SHC 31 – Promote communication in health, social care or children's and young people's settings

Edward

Edward is 36 years old and lives in Nottingham with his mum and dad. He loves communication but finds using spoken words and sentences very difficult. As a child he went to two different special schools where he learnt to use Makaton and Signed English. He also became a good reader. When he left school his speech and language therapist introduced him to a Lightwriter®. This machine uses an electronic voice. Edward really likes his Lightwriter® and can programme it himself. He either types words in, letter by letter, or stores whole sentences and phrases. He especially loves chatting to people and telling them one of the jokes he has stored. The Lightwriter® also has a SIM card in it so he can text-message people. When he is not attending his day centre he loves going on holiday, emailing friends, swimming, and playing snooker, football and bingo. Edward has been described as having autism as well as his speech and language and learning disabilities. For more information about Lightwriter® go to www.tobychurchill.com

Sophie

Sophie is a very friendly and chatty young woman who lives in a supported living scheme in Nottingham, assisted by a team of support workers. She has a fiancé, Steven, and will be moving to a house with him and hopes to get married very soon. Her family, who she describes as 'very nice', live nearby. As well as her mum and dad, she has three sisters and is a proud aunty to a niece and nephew. She enjoys meeting friends and going out for meals or to the pub for a beer (as long as it is real ale and not lager.) Sophie enjoys cooking – especially for her fiancé on a Tuesday evening. She does a range of day activities and her favourite is cricket. She also enjoys going to the gym and watching wrestling. Her favourite music is Marilyn Manson and Eminem, which she likes to play very loud.

Lottie

Lottie is a young woman with a great love for life. She is described as somebody who has profound intellectual and multiple disabilities. She lives in a residential home run by Elizabeth Fitzroy Support. Although she has no speech, she is able to communicate with people who know her well through facial expressions and her body movements – mainly to indicate yes and no. She has very strong views about her likes and dislikes – her bedroom reflects her love of all things pink and girly. She is a member of the 'Recruitment Troop', a group to explore how people with learning disabilities can be involved fully in Elizabeth Fitzroy Support's recruitment process. Together with her keyworker, who has helped to support her communication at group meetings, she has played a powerful part in making sure that people with profound intellectual and multiple disabilities are not forgotten in this process. Lottie loves meeting up with her family and the people she lives with. She has lived with some of these friends for over 19 years and has a good relationship with them all.

Sue

Sue has worked as a speech and language therapist with both children and adults with learning disabilities for 30 years. She has always has a particular interest in the area of complex need, including people with profound and multiple learning disabilities and autistic spectrum conditions. She has been involved in several projects looking at the communication issues associated with important areas such as human rights, safeguarding people with learning disabilities, advocacy and end-of-life care. Sue is now a freelance trainer and consultant and she is active in promoting communication as a human right for all. She has both written and taught about a variety of topics including the Mental Capacity Act. She is also qualified as a Registered Intermediary and works with vulnerable witnesses with learning disabilities in police stations and court. Sue is married and lives in Nottingham. When she's not working, she enjoys craft of all kinds and is involved in her local church.

At the end of the book there is:

A glossary – explaining specialist language in plain English;

An index – to help you look up a particular topic easily.

Study skills

Studying for a qualification can be very rewarding. However, it can be daunting if you have not studied for a long time, or are wondering how to fit your studies into an already busy life. The BILD website contains lots of advice to help you to study successfully, including information about effective reading, taking notes, organising your time, using the internet for research. For further information, go to www.bild.org.uk/qualifications

This unit is one of the mandatory units that everyone doing the full level 2 and level 3 diploma must study. Although anyone studying for the qualifications will find the book useful, it is particularly helpful for people who support a person with a learning disability. The messages and stories used in this book are from people with a learning disability, family carers and people working with them.

Links to assessment

If you are studying for this unit and want to gain accreditation towards a qualification, first of all you will need to make sure that you are registered with an awarding organisation which offers the qualification. Then you will need to provide a portfolio of evidence for assessment. The person responsible for training within your organisation will advise you about registering with an awarding organisation and give you information about the type of evidence you will need to provide for assessment. You can also get additional information from BILD. For more information about qualifications and assessment, go to the BILD website: www.bild.org.uk/qualifications

How this book is organised

Generally each chapter covers one learning outcome from the qualification unit, and one of the Common Induction Standards. The learning outcomes covered are clearly highlighted at the beginning of each chapter. Each chapter starts with a story from a person with a learning disability or family carer or worker. This introduces the topic and is intended to help you think about the topic from their point of view. Each chapter contains:

 Thinking points – to help you reflect on your practice;

Stories – examples of good support from people with learning disabilities and family carers;

 Activities – for you to use to help you to think about your work with people with learning disabilities;

Key points – a summary of the main messages in that chapter;

References and where to go for more information – useful references to help further study.

Introduction

Who is this book for?

Communicating Effectively with People with a Learning Disability is for you if you:

- have a new job working with people with learning disabilities with a support provider or as a personal assistant;

- are a more experienced worker who is studying for a qualification for your own professional development or are seeking more information to improve your practice;

- are a volunteer supporting people with a learning disability;

- are a manager in a service supporting people with a learning disability and you have training or supervisory responsibility for the induction of new workers and the continuous professional development of more experienced staff;

- if you are a direct payment or personal budget user and are planning the induction or training for your personal assistant.

Links to qualifications and the Common Induction Standards

This book gives you all the information you need to complete both one of the Common Induction Standards and the unit on communicating effectively with people with a learning disability from the level 2 and level 3 diplomas in health and social care. You may use the learning from this unit in a number of ways:

- to help you complete the Common Induction Standards;

- to work towards a full qualification e.g. the level 2 or level 3 diploma in health and social care;

- as learning for the unit on communicating effectively for your professional development.

Chapter 1

Understanding why effective communication is important in the work setting

Lottie and her support worker. You should adjust the way you communicate so that people can take the lead and get their message across.

There was one nurse; one of the new nurses wasn't it Lottie? In the morning Lottie likes to sing along to songs and that but he thought she was upset. You have to get used to her sounds and if it means she is happy or sad or whatever. When she's eating – you pull a bit of a funny face, don't you Lottie? – and a lot of people get a bit frightened because it looks like she's struggling and doesn't like the food. But she is enjoying it and you just have to remind her to chew. Communicating whilst she's eating is important otherwise a lot of people kind of give up. Her yes and no is most important definitely – she should be able to choose what drink she wants, when she wants it. It annoys her when people don't ask. They shouldn't assume just because she likes coffee she wants that every time – they should be asking her.

Lottie's key worker

Introduction

Every day we interact with other people in a number of different situations for a whole variety of reasons.

Thinking point

Think about the time from getting up in the morning to arriving at work. How many times did you need to communicate with others? How many times did you need to speak or listen, read or write?

Most of the time, we express ourselves and listen to others with ease. We don't think twice about the complexity of day-to-day communication. We take it for granted. People with learning disabilities, however, often find it challenging to understand and express themselves using verbal (using words) and non-verbal (not using words) communication. It is often up to us to adjust the way we communicate, so that people can take the lead, get their own message across and understand what we say. To respect people, you must make the effort to understand them as people. You need to find out the ways in which they wish to communicate. This takes time and commitment.

> People with learning disabilities have a right under the Disability Discrimination Act to be given communication support. If they do not get it, they are being discriminated against. It is not a case of being nice to people, there is an absolute right to this kind of support.
>
> *Report to the Scottish Government, 2009*

Learning outcomes

This chapter will help you to:

- explain how communication affects all aspects of your work, including relationships;
- identify the different reasons people communicate.

About communication

Communication is vital to us all as human beings. It enables us to socialise with others and make sense of what's going on around us. If we cannot speak, understand words, or read and write very well, we are often excluded, unless others around us are prepared to change. If we are unable to communicate for any reason, we can feel misunderstood, frustrated, isolated, and anxious.

Activity

If you were to pack an imaginary suitcase with everything you needed to communicate, what would you put in it? Remember to think about having something to say, a reason to say it, a way to say it, a person to say it to and a way to understand others' communication.

If you have done the activity, your 'suitcase' will be bulging with things we need in order to communicate – all things that those of us who find communication easy take for granted. You will also realise that many of the things you need are not things over which you have direct control. This is because communication is a shared activity and is about far more than the ability to speak.

When looking at how well communication is working for a person you support, you need to look not just at them, but at what has been called the 'Means, reasons and opportunities' model of communication.

Communication is both verbal and non-verbal. For many people with learning disabilities, verbal communication (using spoken or written words) can be difficult. Non-verbal ways of communicating (including gesture, body language, signing, symbols, objects of reference and other communication aids) are important ways in which many people communicate.

Communication is a two-way activity, involving understanding as well as expressing. How much somebody is able to understand is often misjudged by other people. It is important for you to establish as far as possible how much the people you support understand, so that they can be supported to take a full part in communication.

Communication is a shared activity – dependent on both 'speaker' and 'listener'. It is not enough to focus just on the person with learning disabilities. You must also think about your own communication abilities and if necessary develop new styles, ways and skills of interaction.

Communication can be easily misunderstood. It is easy to misunderstand what somebody is telling us – particularly if they don't use ways of communication with which we are familiar. You will need to be aware of this in your conversations and look for ways to understand better.

Means, reasons and opportunities

(adapted from the original model by Money and Thurman)

You need all three elements to work together if you are going to have effective communication.

Means (how the person communicates) – can the person use their preferred means of communication? Are all means of communication understood and welcomed by the people they meet? Does the person understand the means of communication used by others?

Reasons (why the person communicates) – is the person able to use communication for a wide range of reasons that lead to a fulfilling life? Do other people listen to them when they do this? Do they have the means of communication they need to achieve the reasons they wish to express?

Opportunities (where, when and with whom the person communicates) – does the person have a supportive communication environment? Are they given the time and respect they need to be able to be effective communicators? Do others understand and share their communication styles and methods?

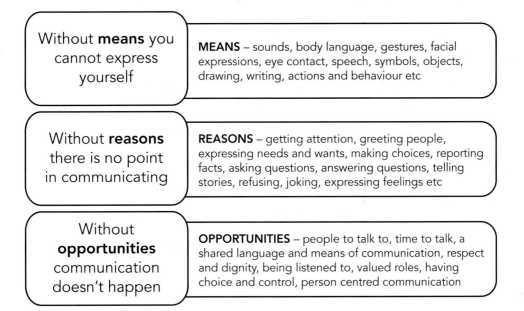

Without **means** you cannot express yourself	**MEANS** – sounds, body language, gestures, facial expressions, eye contact, speech, symbols, objects, drawing, writing, actions and behaviour etc
Without **reasons** there is no point in communicating	**REASONS** – getting attention, greeting people, expressing needs and wants, making choices, reporting facts, asking questions, answering questions, telling stories, refusing, joking, expressing feelings etc
Without **opportunities** communication doesn't happen	**OPPORTUNITIES** – people to talk to, time to talk, a shared language and means of communication, respect and dignity, being listened to, valued roles, having choice and control, person centred communication

Reasons for communication

Everyone communicates for many different reasons.

Edward using his Lightwriter®.

- It is the way we express who we are and how people get to know us.

- It is the way we express our feelings, thoughts and emotions.

- It is the way we express preferences and make choices.

- It is the way we build relationships and make friends.

- It is the way we gain and pass on knowledge and information.

- It is the way we control our lives and develop independence.

People can communicate these reasons in many different ways. They may use words or they may use non-verbal ways, including their behaviour.

Edward communicates using words that are not always easy to understand, Makaton signs, gestures and with a **Lightwriter®**. Look how he is able to use all three methods together to answer questions in this conversation.

Ready? **Hello my name is Edward**

What are the different ways you like to communicate Edward?

Help talk Help talk

What helps you to talk?

Points lighter **Lightwriter®** (points)

And what can you do with your Lightwriter®?

Jokes!

Go on tell me a joke!

Did you hear about the flea that won the lottery?

Er no

He bought a dog in Spain!

(Groans) How do you put jokes in there?

Memory (gestures) **Make joke – save – memory**

Have I got this right? You make up a joke – type the joke in – press save and put it in the memory. Is that it?

Yeah (smiles)

How many jokes are in there?

Hundred

What else do you use it for?

Meal – staff – fish chip

So you can tell the staff what you want! I can remember going out with you ...

Drink – **cappuccino**

Yes we went for a drink and you took all the orders! Anything else you use it for – like when people can't sign with you?

No sign – **talk** (pointed at Lightwriter®)

Ah so when people can't sign you talk using your Lightwriter®?

Yeah (thumbs up)

Anything else?

Address address

When do you need to do that?

Taxi **(taxi)**

Think about a recent conversation you have with somebody you support. Are there any differences in the ways you express these reasons for communicating? Do you notice anything about the reasons you both use in your conversations?

	You	The person you support
Gaining attention		
Expressing your wants or needs		
Asking for information		
Giving information to somebody		
Making choices or expressing preferences		
Refusing or protesting		
Expressing feelings and emotions		
Making jokes		

Why is communication important?

Communication is crucial to our ability to take our place as valued members of society. Many people believe communication should be seen as an important human right. Communication is important in enjoying life, in expressing what you want and don't want, in expressing who you are and in making relationships. Communication is vital to being able to have the kind of life you want and being in control of what happens to you.

Communication is central to being shown respect and treated with dignity by others. This is especially important for people with learning disabilities.

People who cannot speak, understand words, or read or write very well, are undervalued in society. They are automatically excluded unless the people around them are prepared to change. For many years people with learning disabilities have been excluded from mainstream society. Having a voice through effective communication is one way to challenge this. The way you communicate with the people you support is important because it demonstrates how you value this important human right.

> Everyone has a human right to influence, through communication, what happens to them in their lives. Everyone has a human right to be communicated with in ways that are meaningful, understandable and culturally and linguistically appropriate.
>
> *American Bill of Communication Rights, ASHA, 1992*

It is important for you to develop effective ways of communication with the people you support because it will enable you to build up trust in your relationship and support them to achieve a fulfilling life.

Want to know more? Take a look at the BILD guide: *Communication is a human right* (BILD, 2009).

Communication in the work setting

We have already looked at why it is important for you to use effective communication with the people you support, but they are not the only people with whom you need to communicate.

Colleagues

You will almost always be working as a part of a team. The way in which you communicate with your colleagues and family carers is really important in providing good support. You will need to communicate well in order to:

- build good relationships and trust with your colleagues and with family carers;
- learn from their experience and knowledge;
- share important information to make sure you work as a team.

You may not always choose your colleagues as friends outside work, but you will need to work in a professional manner with them whilst you are at work. Good communication is vital to this. When you communicate with colleagues, you must:

- remember the rules about confidentiality;
- think about what you need to tell them to ensure effective support for the person you work with;
- think about the best way to give them the information (face to face, phone, email, written, etc);
- never pass on unfounded rumour or gossip.

Managers and supervisors

Another important form of communication you will take part in at work is with your supervisor or manager. You will learn more about this in the book on personal development in this series. It is important that you and your manager agree the channels of communication you will use and that these work for both of you. They could include:

- supervision meetings;
- appraisals;
- informal feedback;
- face-to-face and telephone contact;
- written records.

The family and friends of the person you support

For very many people with a learning disability their family have been the main constant source of love and support in their life. Family carers often know the person best and many have a wealth of knowledge and information that they would be willing to share with workers. Many people will still be living with their family or, if they are living elsewhere, are regularly in touch with them. You must work in partnership with the person's family to promote the best interest of the person you support and always communicate in a timely and respectful manner, as you would with other care partners.

Outside agencies

Many people with learning disabilities have people from a number of different agencies involved in their lives. This is especially true if they have a lot of medical or other complex needs. People can come from a variety of agencies including health and social care.

Thinking point

How many agencies do you regularly have contact with in your work?

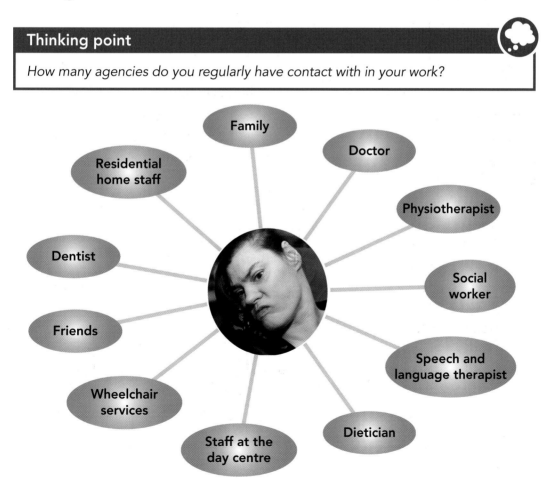

Example of people working with Lottie.

It is important that the person with learning disabilities is not lost in the midst of all the communication between different people involved in their support. You will need to work hard to make sure that however you communicate with people from other agencies, the person is always kept central to your thinking. You will have to use a variety of ways to communicate. This could include:

- face-to-face in conversation;
- face-to-face in meetings;
- by telephone;
- by email or fax;
- by written letter or report.

This communication is important if everyone is to support the person effectively. It helps to prevent:

- important information or actions being missed or becoming lost;
- people repeating things already done by others;
- people thinking somebody else has already done something when they haven't.

It is important that regular contact is maintained and that information shared is understood by everyone. Never be afraid to ask for an explanation if somebody uses jargon you don't understand.

You will learn more about sharing of information with outside agencies in **Chapter 3**.

Key points from this chapter

- We all have a right to communicate and to communication support.

- We all need a means to communicate, a reason to communicate and opportunities to communicate with others.

- It is important to communicate effectively with the people with a learning disability you support and also with colleagues and other care partners such as family carers and workers from other organisations.

References and where to go for more information

References

Money, D and Thurman, S (2002) Inclusive Communication – coming soon near you? *Speech and Language Therapy in Practice*, autumn 2002, 4–5 (www.speechmag.com)

National Joint Committee for the Communicative Needs of Persons with Severe Disabilities (1992) *Guidelines for Meeting the Communication Needs of Persons with Severe Disabilities.* ASHA, 34(Suppl. 7), 2–3

The Scottish Government (May 2009) *Adults with Learning Disabilities and the Criminal Justice System: Their rights and responsibilities:* Report of a summit held in Glasgow on 27 October 2008

Thurman, S (2009) *Communication is a Human Right.* Kidderminster: BILD

Chapter 2

Meeting the communication and language needs, wishes and preferences of individuals

When I first started I'd never worked anywhere like this before so you are quite petrified to be totally honest because it's completely different and quite scary really ... I wasn't looking at it as a barrier but I was worried I was going to get things wrong because I wouldn't be able to understand so learning from other staff definitely is a key thing. I think it's like practice makes perfect isn't it – you kind of have to keep going and practise how you communicate with a certain person.

With Lottie it was quite hard because she obviously likes to get to know people – and it's like every day you have to make the extra effort to come in, just to go through everything, communicate and then it's trust. It takes time, yes. Reading her folders – finding out about her healthwise and stuff like that, likes and dislikes, how she communicates – it all helps you in communicating. I've been her key worker three and a half years – now it's like easy! It's like me and you are having a conversation. That's how it feels when I am having a conversation with Lottie to be honest because of the time we've spent together and part of it is you have really got to get to know someone because they have to trust you. It's definitely natural now.

Lottie's key worker

Introduction

You learnt a little about how communication works and the different ways in which people may communicate in **Chapter 1**. In order to be effective in your communication with the people you support, it is important to recognise the personal communication needs and preferences of that person.

Thinking point

How could you go about establishing the communication preferences of somebody like Lottie who doesn't use words to communicate?

Finding out preferences

There are different ways you can do this, importantly starting with getting to know the person themselves really well.

Asking the person

Of course the obvious starting point is to ask the person themselves how they wish you to communicate with them. Some people will be able to tell you this themselves. However, not everybody will be able to answer this question so you need to take time to find out in different ways. One approach suggests you should go SLOW.

Share activities	One of the best ways to get to know a person and their communication is to spend time with them doing things that they like to do. Try to share the activity and not take over – you will learn a lot more that way.
Listen to the person	Listening will involve more than your ears. As we learnt in **Chapter 1**, a lot of communication is not spoken and so you will need to watch what they may be saying with their body language and behaviour as well as the words they speak.
Observe behaviour	Taking time to watch how the person reacts to different situations and people is helpful to give you an idea about what kind of communicator the person may be. It may also give you some clues as to what they understand of what others say to them.
Wait for the person to communicate	Many people are prevented from communicating effectively because we step in too soon and do not give them the time to communicate. Stepping back and watching what happens will give you a lot of information about the person's communication.

(Adapted from Allow Me *by Irma D Ruiter, 2000)*

Talking to others

People who know the person well may be able to help you to learn how to communicate well with the people you support. Speaking to family, experienced staff and familiar friends will give you clues about how the person likes to communicate. Be aware, however, that sometimes people get it wrong. Always check out what you have been told and compare opinions. Using the forms in the book '*See what I mean*' (see the end of this chapter) is one way you can do this.

Using information

There may be information about the person that will tell you more about their communication preferences. A lot of people now have a communication passport (see later in this chapter) that provides such a guide to communicating effectively with them. If the person has a person centred plan, this should include information about how they like to communicate. A number of person centred thinking tools can be used to record this information. There is more about this in the book on person centred support in this series, *Person Centred Approaches when Supporting People with a Learning Disability*.

Someone's culture is not simply about the language they use or the way they dress – it's about much more than that, it defines what people believe and the way they think, feel and behave.

Thinking about culture

To get to know somebody well you must also appreciate their cultural preferences and needs. Someone's culture is not simply about the language they use or the way they dress. It's much more than that – it defines what people believe and the way they think, feel and behave. It can be influenced by their ethnic origin, religion, gender, family relationships, social experiences and much more. It is important to be aware that aspects of communication differ between cultures. It is important not to simply apply cultural stereotypes but to get to know the person as an individual, so you can identify how this affects:

- their communication preferences and needs;

- their interpretation and understanding of your communication;

- how you communicate together.

Language differences

The person with a learning disability and their family may speak a different language from you, or they may speak one language at home and a different one when they're attending a day service or other activity. Even coming from a different part of the country may mean that a different dialect is used which can cause confusion or even offence. For example, terms of endearment, such as 'love' and 'me duck', are acceptable in some parts of the UK but offensive in others. Being told you are 'bonnie' means you are pretty in some places, but that you are rather plump in others.

Some people find it easy to switch between languages, but others find it difficult. Some people may be more skilled in one than the other and therefore need important information given to them in their stronger language. Sometimes it isn't possible to translate literally from one language into another. This may be because there are no equivalent words or because the idea itself may play an unimportant part in the culture or be contradictory to the values of the culture.

Non-verbal communication differences

It's not only verbal communication where there can be cultural differences. Non-verbal cues vary between cultures and can lead to misinterpretation. For example, amongst some Hindu communities, folding your arms is a sign of humility. In a Western culture this could be a sign of stubbornness or aggression. Lack of eye contact is seen as a barrier to communication or even a sign of deceitfulness in some Western cultures. However, Somali children are taught not to make eye contact with adults. Pictures and photographs can have different meanings in different cultures so you need to think about the cultural meaning of images that you use.

Written information

If information is not available in your language, you may miss out on important information or services. Some languages don't have written scripts. For example, Mirpuri is a spoken but not written dialect of Punjabi. Some people may not be able to understand written information because of their poor reading skills. You must never make the assumption that simply providing information in somebody's own language is the best way to pass on information. Find out from the person how they would like to receive information – it could be spoken, easy-read, video or audio, for example. If you use pictorial information of any type, make sure you use a range of images that reflect the whole community.

Cultural differences

You should always become aware of important cultural values held by the person you support and their family. Different cultures can have different concepts of disability, which can lead to misunderstandings. Your place of work may have a different ethos and atmosphere to the one the person experiences with their family. It is important to know what values are important for them.

For example, a person from an orthodox Jewish background would have special requirements for prayers, food and cleanliness. A person with strong Christian beliefs might find a Halloween party offensive. Find out all you can about the person so you understand what really matters to them. Consider making contact with community leaders. This will have a positive impact on how you support and communicate with them.

Thinking point

Consider whether you have noticed any cultural differences in spoken and non-spoken communication with the people you support. Have you ever misinterpreted these? Do you ever talk to the person you support or their families about cultural differences?

How I like my support workers to talk to me

I like my support workers to talk to me really nicely, friendly, lots of talking and they say 'what have you been up to?' Speak clearly, like slow when they talk. They think what they're going to say and they look at me. When I say something back to them, I look at them. If they want something, I look at them. Simple words. I ask them about say it again if sometimes I get confused. Say it again if I haven't understood. I just tell them straight! I don't want supporters to be grumpy, miserable, nasty, talking down on the floor, muttering. My supporters help at the doctors. Doctors need good listening. My supporters go in and make sure I am all right, like, am I comfy with it? Sometimes they write it in a notebook what I need to have or if I need to say something about something or sometimes I change my mind. Sometimes I forget what I've said. It's their job!

Sophie

Effective communication

There is no simple rule book about how to communicate effectively with the person you support. Each person is an individual and will need you to communicate in a way that suits them. There are some helpful principles for you to consider.

Think about your spoken communication

Sophie and a support worker: I like my support workers to talk to me really nicely, friendly, lots of talking and they say 'What have you been up to?'

It is helpful to match the types of words and sentences you use to the person's ability, understanding and experience. Do they understand the words you are using? Can they understand the questions you ask? Do they need you to shorten and simplify your sentences? Try not to bombard them with questions as this can lead people to 'clam up'. It is always better to keep your language simple without being patronising. If the person doesn't seem to understand what you are trying to tell them, there are lots of things you can try – just make sure you do one at a time or you could confuse them further.

If the person you are supporting doesn't understand you then you could try the following.

- Communicating more slowly and clearly and repeating what you have said.

- Allowing the person more time to understand – maybe give them time to think about what you have said and then come back to them for a response.

- Simplifying what you've said using shorter sentences and fewer words.

- Thinking more about your non-verbal communication. Avoid your body language saying something different from your words which will confuse the person.

- Checking the person understands the vocabulary you are using. Are they familiar with the ideas you are talking about?

- Supporting what you're saying with signs or pictures as appropriate.

- Using different ways to give the information such as drawing or showing what you mean by demonstration.

- Thinking about whether the environment is too noisy or distracting or whether you need to try at a different time of day when the person is more alert.

- Thinking about whether you are the best person to give this message – would someone else be better?

Think about the person's spoken communication

Sometimes what a person says and what they mean can be different things. Make sure you look at the whole situation before you decide what they are saying. And check out your interpretation. If you don't understand what someone is trying to tell you – don't panic! You may find that when you are supporting a person there are occasions when you won't fully understand what they are trying to communicate. It is never a good idea to just pretend that you understand. If you ask them to repeat their communication, apologise for not understanding and never blame them for not communicating clearly. You could say something like, *I'm sorry, I'm having difficulty understanding what you said. Can you help me by saying it again?* Or you could ask them to *Show me.* You could also ask a colleague or one of their family or friends who might know the person better to help you understand. You could also use pictures or signs – the person may be able to point or sign more easily than speak. Take your time and be creative. Give the person time to express themselves in other ways.

Think about your non-verbal communication

You need to be aware of your own non-verbal communication as this will often be very important in helping the people you support to understand you. This will include your facial expressions, eye contact, body language and gestures. People who find spoken words difficult often rely on your non-verbal communication. Make sure you use it well to convey your meaning. You should maximise your use of facial expression, gesture and eye contact, along with any props such as objects or pictures to make clear what you are saying. Having an object or picture about the subject of your conversation will often help a person to remember what it is you are talking about. Always remember to think about the person with whom you are communicating. Some people with autism, for example, find direct eye contact painful. For some people the use of touch, such as a hand on their shoulder, is an important way of making contact with them. For others such touch might be distressing.

Think about the person's non-verbal communication

Pay close attention to a person's non-spoken communication as this is a good way to understand how the person is feeling. Remember that sometimes eyes and faces can communicate something different from what is being said. Remember that somebody's non-spoken communication can be very individual to them. For example, usually people maintain eye contact if they want to communicate and are interested in what is happening or being discussed. Lack of eye contact can mean the person is unhappy or depressed or unwilling to communicate at that time. However, some people with autism find establishing and maintaining eye contact very difficult, so you will need to know the person well before you can truly understand their communication. Another example is body posture. People who have their legs or arms crossed usually feel withdrawn or unhappy whereas people who show an open body posture are usually more comfortable and calm. But there are cultural issues relating to body language and you need to understand the person's background and earlier experiences before you can really understand their body language.

Think about the setting

Communication does not just involve two people. You will also need to consider the time and place of the communication and whether they are helpful or not. There are many questions you could ask yourself to check this out. You can probably think of more.

Lois signing to her neighbour. Communication does not just involve two people. Think also about the time and place of the communication and whether they are helpful or not.

- Do we have enough time for this conversation?
- Are we comfortable? What about the furniture, temperature, lighting? Is the room layout helpful for conversation? Does it feel relaxed?
- Am I sitting at the right level to talk to the person? Can we see each other easily? Are there any distractions such as music, TV or other people?
- Does the person have any particular needs? What about glasses, hearing aids, communication aids?

- Is this the right time of day for this conversation? Is the person alert? Do they have any other important commitments at this time? How long can they concentrate? How often should we take a break?

- Do I have a good relationship with this person? Do we know each other well? How can we get to know each other better?

- Could other people be helpful in this conversation? What about an interpreter, family member or close friend?

Think about total or inclusive communication

The use of total or inclusive communication where all means of communication are valued and used as appropriate is a vital part of working with many people with a learning disability. It is one of the best ways to promote effective communication.

Total communication is a nationally recognised process of using speaking with body language, facial expression, multi-sensory channels, objects, representational objects, photographs, pictures, symbols, writing, videos, computers as appropriate for individual understanding and expression of needs, wants, choices, independence. Anything that promotes more effective two-way communication!

Somerset Total Communication

Communicating effectively with people with learning disabilities requires both creativity and reflection. There are many communication strategies, tools and approaches that can be used to promote effective communication. It is important to remember that none of these is appropriate for everybody and there are no easy shortcuts to finding out how someone may be feeling or what they may be telling you. Find out about these forms of communication from the person you support or their family or seek advice from a colleague with experience. It is often wise to seek advice from a speech and language therapist in considering which approach is suitable for any individual.

There are lots of different ways to communicate – there is information about where to find out more about these approaches at the end of the chapter. Here is a summary of some of the ways you may come across.

Using information about someone's communication

There are many ways of gathering and recording information about how best to communicate with a person. They can be a useful way to get to know somebody and to make sure everyone can communicate effectively with them.

All about me or life history books are personal histories that can develop a sense of identity and provide a focus for conversation about topics of interest.

Communication passports or dictionaries are guides to communicating with and supporting somebody effectively. They can be in book form or produced in a multi media way on CD or DVDs. Person-centred thinking tools used in person-centred plans can also be a good way to record information about communication.

Sensory and creative approaches

For some people with very complex communication needs, words and other formal means of communication have little meaning. Using body language, sensory interaction and other creative ways to communicate can be highly effective.

Intensive interaction is an effective and practical approach to interacting with people through sharing their own language. It uses body, voice and your presence to develop communicative exchanges in ways suited to each person.

Communication using senses can help people to receive information through sensations such as touch, sound, smell and sight. This can be done using everyday objects in daily life or in special environments such as multi-sensory rooms. Dance, drama, art and music can also help self-expression and emotional well-being, done as a leisure activity or offered as therapy by qualified therapists.

Augmentative or alternative communication (AAC)

Some people are helped by additional means of communication if they have not developed enough spoken communication to meet their needs or need help to understand words.

Objects of reference can be used to represent words and ideas and are often used for people who cannot either see or understand pictures. For example, showing a person a mug to ask whether they want a drink of tea.

Using an object of reference.

Signs are hand gestures that are used in an agreed way to communicate. Signs from British Sign Language (BSL) have been used in several vocabularies specifically for people with learning disabilities such as Makaton and Signalong.

Signing.

Pictures can be in the form of photographs, drawings or symbols. They can be added to written information to make this more accessible or understandable for people with learning disabilities. They can also be used with individuals to help them make choices, or to understand events that will happen that day. A variety of symbols and picture banks have been specially developed for use with people with learning disabilities. If these are used in the organisation you work for, you should be given training in how to use them properly.

Using pictures as a reference.

Communication aids can range from simple boards or books to more sophisticated 'talking aids'. These electronic aids can be operated via eye gaze, switches, keyboards or touch screens to trigger spoken messages.

A BIGmack communication aid.

Individual approaches

Taking a truly person-centred approach to communication means that for some people there may be individual approaches needed to meet their particular needs and preferences. This can include obtaining independent advocacy support. This can involve supporting the person to speak up for themselves or non-instructed advocacy, which is where an advocate takes positive action on behalf of a person who is unable to give a clear indication of their views or wishes. A number of specialised approaches are also available. A popular one is Talking Mats™.

This can help people think and express their opinions using sets of picture symbols attached to a mat. Another is Social Stories™, where a short story is written in a special way to provide social information to people with autistic spectrum conditions.

Easy-read information

If information is to be meaningful, it ideally needs to be made accessible by tailoring it to the communication needs of the person. This means using 'easy-read' language in simple sentences and can also involve the use of pictures, photos or symbols as appropriate. There is a growing amount of information available as books and leaflets and on websites designed to make complicated information easier for people to understand. For more information you may find *Making Written Information Easier to Understand for People with Learning Disabilities* (from the Department of Health) helpful in thinking more about using and making easy-read documents.

> **Activity**
>
> *Would a person you support benefit from any of the above approaches? Take some time to find out more about the approach and then discuss with the person concerned or with your colleagues. Discuss how one of the approaches above may or may not be helpful.*

Responding to communication

When you are supporting a person with learning disabilities it is important to watch closely their reactions to situations. Interpreting these reactions is part of your role as a responsive communication partner. This is especially important where people find it difficult to express clearly how they are feeling.

We all feel frustrated and hurt sometimes when we can't communicate what we want to say, or when we misunderstand what others have told us. Despite our frustration, we can usually do something when communication breaks down. We can usually repair the breakdown by saying, *What do you mean by…?* and *What I meant was…* Many people with learning disabilities have had little opportunity to develop these skills. Where communication is less developed, as with people who have a severe or profound disability, they may have few opportunities to express their feelings and thoughts or to respond to what is happening to them. In situations like this it's possible that people use their behaviour as a way to express their feelings.

Thinking point

Think about a time when someone you were talking to did not seem to understand the point you were trying to make, or when they did not seem to hear you properly. How did you feel? Did you show your feelings? If so, how?

If you are anxious because the world feels like a very threatening and unpredictable place or you can't get your message across clearly to others, it is likely that you might find other ways to express yourselves, for example:

- grabbing things (instead of asking);
- pushing (instead of waiting or saying *Excuse me*);
- hitting (instead of saying *Please don't do that*);
- screaming (instead of asking *Can we do something different now?*).

It is helpful to ask yourself if there are hidden messages when somebody behaves in such ways rather than simply labelling them as 'challenging'. One way to remember some of these messages is to think SEAT.

Is the person seeking Stimulation?
I'm bored. I need something meaningful to do.

Does the person want to Escape?
I want to get out of this task/place/noise/company. I want to stop. I don't understand what you want, the anxiety's unbearable.

Does the person want some Attention

I need some undivided attention, some personal interest. I need someone to belong to. I feel insecure.

Is this a request for something Tangible

I'm hungry/thirsty/tired/cold/in pain. I want the music off/the TV on. My mother hasn't come, I'm disappointed and angry.

(From Challenge to Change: Better Services for People with Challenging Behaviour. *Mary Myers, 1995*)

Communicating in sensitive situations

You will often find yourself communicating with the people whom you support in sensitive situations. For example, going with someone to the doctor or supporting someone who is upset. Or when you provide intimate personal care or talk to someone about confidential matters. In these situations you will need to ensure that the person you are supporting is at the centre of what you are doing and that you do everything you can to understand and promote their needs and wishes. How you handle a sensitive situation can have a long-term effect on how the person feels and reacts and on their relationship with you, so you should pay particular attention to your communication.

You should keep in mind the following good practice ideas.

- Listen carefully to what the person is telling you and reflect back what the person has told you. *This shows respect. Reflecting back the key points of the conversation can reassure the person you have correctly understood what they are telling you.*

- Think about where you talk to the person. It is often best to look for a quiet place where you will not be overheard. *This shows that you know confidentiality and privacy are important and helps the person to feel more confident to talk to you.*

- Take your time and communicate in a way that is most suitable for the person. Watch carefully for the person's responses, in both their verbal and non-verbal communication. *This shows you are working in a person-centred way and respecting the person's communication and emotional needs.*

- If possible, check with the person some while later to see whether they have understood everything or have thought of more points they want to discuss. *This gives an opportunity to check the understanding of the person involved as well as your own understanding. It also gives an opportunity to raise any other issues.*

Communication is everybody's responsibility

Good communication is all about respecting the person and taking a person centred approach. The support needed will vary from person to person, but the evidence of totally person centred inclusive communication will be apparent by a clear 'Yes' to each of the statements included in the diagram below.

Whatever communication methods (verbal or non verbal) work best for me are used and valued by me and others who communicate with me

Person Centred Inclusive Communication

Whatever communication tools, techniques or technology I need are freely available to me throughout my life without professional, financial or commercial barriers

My communication partners (family, friends, supporters and others) are trained, willing and able to communicate effectively with me

The places I go to are able to support my communication needs and are adapted as necessary to enable me to communicate well

My communication partners understand and value my communication, listen to me and take time to support my communication

I get the professional and personal support I need to enable me to communicate to my full potential

Policies and strategies that affect me take into account my communication and include me in appropriate ways

Activity

Take a copy of this diagram to your next staff meeting and discuss it with your colleagues. How well do you think your team is doing at providing this kind of person centred inclusive communication for the people you support?

Support for communication

Some of the people you support will benefit from the extra support of specialist services to enable them to communicate effectively. Such services include:

- translation and interpretation services;
- advocacy services;

- easy-read information services;
- speech and language therapy.

You will learn more about how to work with these services in **Chapter 3**.

Key points from this chapter

- Find out about the person's communication preferences.
- You can use shared activities, listening to the person, observation and waiting for the person to communicate as ways of finding out about how a person communicates.
- Personal barriers to communication can be because of an impairment or illness such as a hearing loss or memory problem, a difficulty in finding the right words or being physically able to speak or difficulties in being in social situations.
- Social barriers to communication can include low expectations, lack of time, lack of focus or removing the need for the person to communicate; this is called pre-empting.
- Physical barriers to communication can include being physically uncomfortable or in pain, a noisy or distracting environment, stress or tiredness.
- Cultural barriers to communication can arise when the worker doesn't appreciate the cultural differences in communicate with the person they support.
- It is important to get advice and support to help the person communicate from advocacy services or from a translator, interpreter or speech and language therapist as required.

References and where to go for more information

References

BILD (2009) *Hearing from the Seldom Heard* www.bild.org.uk

Department of Health (2010) *Making Written Information Easier to Understand for People with Learning Disabilities. Guidance for People who Commission or Produce Easy Read Information.* Revised edition 2010. www.dh.gov.uk

Goldbart, J and Caton, S (2010) *Communication and People with the Most Complex Needs: What works and why this is essential.* London: Mencap

Grove, N (2000) *See What I Mean: Guidelines to aid understanding of communication by people with severe and profound learning disabilities.* Kidderminster: BILD

Hewitt, H (2006) *Life Story Books for People with Learning Disabilities: A practical guide.* Kidderminster: BILD

Mencap (2009) *Your Guide to Communicating with People with a Learning Disability.* London: Mencap

Millar, S with Aitkin, S (2003) *Personal Communication Passports: Guidelines for good practice.* Edinburgh: CALL centre

Myers, M (1995) *Challenge to Change: Better services for people with challenging behaviour,* in Philpot, T and Ward, L (1995) *Values and Visions; Changing ideas in services for people with learning difficulties.* Butterworth Heinemann

Nind, M and Hewett, D (2001) *A Practical Guide to Intensive Interaction.* Kidderminster: BILD

Ruiter, ID (2000) *Allow Me: A guide to promoting communication skills in adults with developmental delays.* Ontario: Hanen Centre

Websites

Equality and Human Rights Commission www.equalityhumanrights.com For *How to Use Easy Read Words and Pictures*

Oxfordshire Total Communication www.oxtc.co.uk Information and links to all types of alternative methods of communication

Gloucestershire Total Communication www.totalcommunication.org.uk Information and links to all types of alternative methods of communication

Chapter 3

Overcoming barriers to communication

Elizabeth Fitzroy Support wanted to find out how to include people with learning disabilities more fully in the whole of their recruitment and interviewing process. So they set up the 'recruitment troop'. People who used their services came to a number of meetings to give their views. Lottie was invited to attend as she has strong views about her likes and dislikes. 'We went through the whole recruitment process and we were asked what we thought could change with the application form, how they recruited people in the first place, even the type of questions and how they were asked … all the way through the interview process. We drove down to Milton Keynes – we got free lunch and that was always nice! I would narrow questions down so Lottie could contribute so I'd say 'do you want to say this?' And she would tell me yes or no.

I liked being out on the project with her all day – more time together. I knew her well already but we got a little bit closer. Lottie liked being asked herself – being included rather than it being what we think is best. It was important having Lottie there because one of the things that was being forgotten in job descriptions was about personal care. Other people in the troop said themselves 'I would never have thought about that because it's not one of my needs' but having Lottie there made them think about it. Now the interview process, the application form has all changed and it will help everybody because they will more likely get the right person for the job because of what we did. And Lottie was able to say what she wanted in a support worker.

From a discussion with Lottie's support worker

Introduction

Communication barriers usually arise because there is a breakdown in understanding between the person who is sending the message and those who are meant to be receiving it. There are many reasons why people with learning disabilities face communication barriers and may need support.

Thinking point

Have you ever been on holiday to a country where you couldn't speak, understand or read the language? You may have had difficulty ordering a meal in a restaurant, because you couldn't understand the menu and the waiters didn't speak English. How did it feel to be excluded in that way?

Learning outcomes

This chapter will help you to:

- recognise barriers to effective communication;
- demonstrate ways to overcome barriers to communication;
- demonstrate ways to minimise and clarify misunderstandings;
- explain how to access extra support or services to enable individuals to communicate effectively.

This chapter covers:

- Common Induction Standards – Standard 3 – Communicate effectively: Learning Outcome 3, 1.3
- Level 2 SHC 21 – Introduction to communication: Learning Outcomes 3 and 4
- Level 3 SHC 31 – Promote communication: Learning Outcome 3 (not 3.1)

Personal barriers to communication

People with learning disabilities face a range of personal barriers, from very significant to more subtle difficulties. Personal communication barriers can affect a person's ability to:

- **understand communication from others** – such as having a hearing loss, concentration and memory difficulties, lack of understanding of verbal or non-verbal information;
- **express communication to others** – such as lacking speech, having difficulties in forming words or sentences clearly, difficulty finding the words they need;

- **take part in communication with others** – such as difficulty taking part in conversations or meeting the demands of social situations.

We do not have exact figures for the numbers of people with learning disabilities who face such communication barriers, but the Foundation for People with Learning Disabilities (2000) suggested that it is anywhere from 50 per cent to 90 per cent of people who experience some level of personal barrier to their communication.

> **Activity**
>
> *Spend some time thinking about the personal communication barriers faced by a person you support. Find out some more about these barriers by asking them, their family or other professionals, reading up on them in their records or researching in the library or on the internet. Now imagine you faced these barriers on a daily basis. How would you feel?*

It is important to spot any difficulties with hearing and sight experienced by the people you support. Almost 40 per cent of adults with a learning disability will have a hearing loss, yet for many people this may not be recognised by the people supporting them. If you think a person might be experiencing hearing or sight problems you should support them to seek treatment. If you want to find out more about this, there are helpful references at the end of this chapter.

Those with the most complex personal barriers may have reactive communication. They can only react to real-life situations at the time they are happening. They may indicate their feelings about something through their body language or facial expression, for example. There is always a high degree of 'best-guessing' in interpreting such communication. Some reactive communication is intentional (the person means to use it as communication) whilst some is unintentional (a reflex or reaction to something of which the person isn't consciously aware).

> With Lottie I would say look at her face – her facial expression is key as you can tell if she doesn't like something or if she's bored or if she's just listening or she's happy. Or when she is vocal that is a key thing as that will indicate whether she is happy or sad and I suppose that is just getting used to how she is vocal. If you need to have a conversation with her quickly it's questions – ask her questions – rather than open-ended questions it's yes or no questions for Lottie mostly. To say yes she'll raise one of her hands, she'll squeeze your hand and she

also sticks her tongue out. For no, sometimes she grinds her teeth or grits her teeth together. She can also raise both of her hands and have an unhappy face and cycling her legs – looks like she's riding a bike; that's an extreme no! It's up to us more experienced staff to be there and make suggestions to new staff and as a newcomer you should always ask. Never be frightened to ask questions. I'd rather somebody asked me questions twenty times than have a go and get it wrong.

Lottie's key worker

It is important to use creative and sensory forms of communication and interaction when communicating with reactive communicators.

On the other hand, people who can use proactive communication are able to initiate communication without the need to be tied to the 'here and now' or relying on others. They have the understanding and motivation to do this as well as a way of expressing it. They therefore have more independence in their communication. They may still face barriers if the means and methods they use to communicate their messages are not readily accepted or understood by others.

If you talk to Edward he will tell you he is '*useless talk*'. Don't listen to him – he is a fantastic communicator! He can tell you about how he went to a nursery he got '*banned*' because nobody knew how to communicate with him. Then he went to a school where he leant '*signing – long time ago*'. His next school helped him with his talking and writing and he will tell you about '*Mary – Tuesday and Thursday*' (the days he saw his speech and language therapist). He left school and still '*need help talk*' and his therapist and others helped him to get a Lightwriter®. This has made such a difference to his life. He can program it himself and he carries it with him strapped round his middle in a bag. He still uses words and signs a lot but says his Lightwriter® is '*better – help talk*'. He can do so many things with it. He can tell jokes, ask for food and drink when he's out, tell the taxi driver the address he wants to go to – it even has a SIM card so he can send and receive text messages. His first Lightwriter® lasted for ten years and Edward will tell you he had to be '*very patient*' whilst he waited for his new one to arrive. He has had this for over two years now. Using the Lightwriter® means that his spelling has improved greatly so he can now also keep in touch with people by email too (usually so he can do his favourite thing – tell them a joke).

From a conversation with Edward

The use of **total or inclusive communication** is important in ensuring positive communication with proactive communicators. You learnt more about this and a number of communication approaches in **Chapter 2**.

Despite people facing many personal barriers, the biggest barriers to communication for people with learning disabilities are not in fact these, but rather how others respond and make it possible for effective communication to take place. These barriers can be social or physical.

Social barriers to communication

Day-to-day social situations may make it difficult for a person with learning disabilities to communicate effectively. Many of these barriers are caused by the attitudes of people around them. They can be overcome if you think about the way you work and are creative in the way you support people.

There are some common barriers in the social environment for people with learning disabilities and they can be overcome.

Many barriers can be caused by other people's attitudes. Think about the way you work and be creative in the way you support people.

Low expectations

People's expectations are often so low that they don't involve people with learning disabilities in conversations, thinking they will be unable to understand or that they cannot contribute. You should raise your expectations and always expect and support communication with the person you work with. Value should be placed on whatever way people can contribute, whether spoken or unspoken.

Lack of time

Sometimes we use time as an excuse. We say there is just not enough time to listen to people and don't give them time to communicate adequately. We assume the person can't express themselves, and we say everything for them. Instead you should give the person you support time to communicate. Never interrupt and always give people the time they need to complete what they want to say. This shows respect for the person and what they want to communicate.

Lack of focus

Sometimes we are so preoccupied with our own affairs that we don't attend to what someone is trying to tell us. We often ignore a person's attempts to communicate. Other times we hear what is being said, but don't really listen or concentrate on what this means for the person concerned. You must be person centred. This is important every day in your support of a person with a learning disability. In all you do you should respect the person you support and promote their views and wishes, not your own.

Pre-empting

Sometimes, without realising it, we remove the need for people to communicate and therefore reduce the opportunities the people we support have for positive communication. Not all pre-empting is wrong. For example, predictable routines can help somebody with autism to reduce their anxiety, and ready access to possessions and activities can increase independence. However, if somebody is not having the opportunity to exercise choice and control because they are constantly being pre-empted, it can be good to alter their environment or your communication to create more opportunities. You can do this in a variety of ways (see table).

What is pre-empting?	Reducing pre-empting
Physical pre-empting removes the need to communicate because of the surroundings or routine. For example, possessions always being in the same place and readily accessible or set daily routines such as meals, work patterns, etc.	• Create opportunities in the day for co-operation and joint activities.
Non-verbal pre-empting removes the need to communicate because other people take control. For example 'Come on; we're going swimming now' or 'Do you want a drink?' (holding out a cup). Here all the person has to do is respond by action (getting up to go swimming or taking the cup).	• Provide plenty of time – it is often quicker if you do something for somebody, but not as valuable for their communication and independence.
	• Show the people you support that you expect a response such as not interrupting; looking at the person expectantly and giving encouraging non-verbal feedback (e.g. head nods, 'mm', etc).

Verbal pre-empting removes the need for communication because of the way the person talks. For example, 'What do you want for dinner – would you like fish?' or 'What did you do last night – did you watch TV?' The answer is almost given for the person.

- Remember people have the right to express themselves as much as they can. Don't take over.

- Think about any routines you have. Why do you do things that way? Who controls things? How can you give more control to the people you support?

- Think about the way you ask questions. Is there any way to make questions more open so the person can say more than just yes or no?

Physical barriers to communication

Sometimes we don't think enough about what it's like for the person who is trying to communicate with us and the effect of the physical environment on communication. There are some situations where it's more difficult to communicate. The table below identifies a number of potentially difficult communication situations and what you can do to support communication in these situations.

Physical barriers to communication	How to overcome physical barriers to communication
Discomfort Being in a place where a person with a learning disability feels uncomfortable may be distracting. It may be too hot or cold or just be a place where they are ill at ease.	**Find a comfortable place** With the person you support, identify places where they feel most comfortable. These will be the best places to communicate effectively.
Noise Being in a noisy environment where there's lots of background noise from piped music, other people talking and telephones ringing can make it difficult to hear what people are saying.	**Choose a quiet environment** Use your observation skills as well as asking the person how they feel about communicating in noisy places. Be led by them in identifying the best places to communicate.

Distractions

Being where there are lots of people around and lots of activity can be distracting and make it more difficult for people to communicate.

Stress

Being in some situations, such as a one-to-one 'interview' situation, can be stressful. Some people can find particular people or places stressful to be around, making it difficult to concentrate on communication.

Tiredness

It is extremely tiring to communicate if you have any difficulties in either expressing yourself or understanding others. Some of the people you support will also take medication which leads them to become less alert at certain times of the day.

Sensory overload

Some people with autistic spectrum condition find dealing with different sensory signals such as sounds and sights very difficult. They can very quickly become overwhelmed by these signals and find it impossible to communicate with other people in this state.

Find a calm atmosphere

Some people love crowds and others hate them. Being person centred in your approach to communication will mean that you will be seeking to find out what the person you support really prefers.

Minimise stress

Make sure you know what factors make a situation stressful for the person you are supporting. Once you know what they are, you can avoid them to create a more relaxing setting in which to communicate.

Take a break

Make sure you know how to spot signs that somebody may be getting tired and suggest a break in the conversation. Choose times of the day when you know the person is most alert, to talk about important things.

Find out what helps

Find out as much as you can about what makes the person comfortable. Be prepared to change things in the environment to help. Get help from a specialist in this area (such as an occupational therapist) if necessary.

Cultural barriers to communication

You learnt about some of the cultural differences that are important to be aware of in **Chapter 2**. None of these needs to be a barrier to communication if they are recognised and taken into account in the way you communicate with the person you support. If you are uncertain about this, go back to **Chapter 2** and take another look at what it says about this.

Physical contact and touch

One important related topic is that of physical contact or touch. You may find physical contact a useful way of communicating with people with learning disabilities or of encouraging them to communicate with you, such as:

- putting your hand on someone's shoulder as you say hello;

- tapping someone lightly to draw their attention;

- catching hold of someone's arm to ask them to wait.

There are times when physical contact is a helpful and appropriate part of communicating. It is particularly important when you are communicating with people, for example, using intensive interaction. There are other times when it definitely isn't. Physical contact is inappropriate when it is intrusive or disrespectful, or when the person does not want physical contact. Communication through physical contact is always inappropriate if it involves pain, sexual intent or unnecessary touching of intimate parts of the body.

One of the best ways to decide whether or not physical contact is appropriate is to be guided by the person and their reactions and by the policy of your organisation. We all differ in the kind of physical contact we feel comfortable with. Often this depends on the experiences we've had and on the situation we are in. Sometimes it depends on what's expected in your culture. As a support worker you'll often be in situations where you use physical contact quite naturally to help with communication. Sometimes, however, someone you are working with will show you quite clearly that they aren't happy or comfortable with what you're doing. They may do this perhaps with a shrug or by pushing you away or by saying quite plainly, 'Don't do that'. It is important to follow their wishes.

Activity

Read your organisation's policy on physical contact and touch. Do they raise any questions for you? Discuss any questions you have with your manager.

Misunderstandings in communication

Misunderstanding with the people you support can easily happen if:

- you don't understand what the person is telling you;

- the person doesn't understand what you are saying;

- either of you don't realise that the other hasn't understood you.

This can happen whether or not the person you are supporting uses words to communicate.

> Because we have worked together for such a long time now we can almost see the connection in each other's face that now she's getting what we're talking about and equally that we are not getting what Sophie is talking about. One or two times we have a conversation where words are getting mixed up and we are coming back to a conversation that we were talking about before – we're talking about two things basically – so we just break it down gradually.
>
> *Sophie's key worker*

Listening to the people you support

Many people think listening is a natural and very easy skill, but most of us could benefit from improving our listening skills. It is all too easy to interrupt people or let our attention wander when others are talking. When you are supporting people who find communication hard, it is important that you respect their communication with you by listening carefully. This means giving them your full attention and trying not to interrupt. It means 'listening with your eyes' by watching their non-verbal communication as well as what they say. It means thinking broadly about what they are telling you. Do you know something about them or their past that helps you to make sense of what they are saying? It can be helpful to listen for the main point the person is trying to get across. Then ask if you can check that you have got it right by telling them what you think they have just said. Never pretend you have understood if you haven't. We looked at some things you could try in such a situation in **Chapter 2**. Encourage the person in the use of total communication in using whatever means they can to get their message across to you. Remember they are more likely to do this if you use total communication too.

Difficulties in understanding

Research has shown that we often misjudge the ability to understand of the people we support. This is probably because understanding is such a complicated process. When we talk about understanding we often think about the words and sentences people use. This is known as **verbal understanding**. People with learning disabilities often find understanding words and sentences more difficult than we imagine. This is for lots of different reasons, including the fact that words often mean different things at different times and in different situations. Think how many different meanings there are when you hear the word 'light' or 'trip'. People may know what individual words mean but find it hard to follow the meaning of sentences. Some idea words are especially difficult. For example, many people with learning disabilities find words related to 'time' difficult (such as before, after, later, next, etc.).

In fact for many people, their difficulty understanding words is disguised, because they make excellent use of what is known as **situational understanding**. Think about when you go abroad and don't speak the language. You can often work out what people are saying if you look for clues in the situation (such as their tone of voice, their gestures, your previous experience of similar situations, what other people are doing, and any other visual clues you can see). This is what many people with learning disabilities do – they look around them and then make an informed guess as to what you may be saying, perhaps backed up by being able to understand one or two words you are saying.

There is also something we could call **hidden meaning**. Take as an example the saying 'I'm going to hit the sack': you may understand the words in the sentence, but to show full understanding you have to know what those words mean when they are in a sentence together – and that is sometimes hidden. We sometimes only hint at what we wish to say – perhaps because we are being sarcastic or are using non-literal sayings or simply because we are communicating in an indirect or vague way.

Thinking point

Think about the following sayings.

'I'll see you in a minute'

'You crack me up'   *'I'm your biggest fan!'*

'Pull your socks up'   *'You are a real lady killer'*

'Don't butter me up'   *'Many hands make light work'*

What kind of confusion can you imagine arising from these expressions?

In order to make sense of what is said to us we all use a mixture of ways to understand.

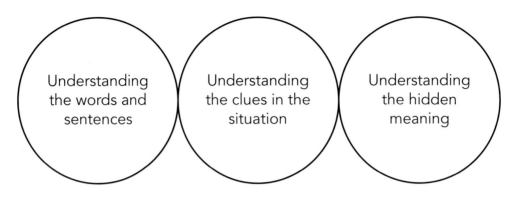

Think about these three areas when you are working out what the person you support understands.

In addition, there are lot of **real-life factors** that will impact on how well any of us understand what someone says. Things like:

- how tired we are;
- how worried or anxious we are;
- how interested in the subject we are;
- whether we like the person who is telling us;
- how well we are feeling.

Thinking point

How often have you heard people say 'He understands everything I say to him!' Can this be true?

Helping the people you support to understand

There are lots of different ways you can do this. One of the most important ways is to find out as much as you can about what the person can understand and what they find more difficult. Watch and listen to the person carefully. You will often find out more from what the person does than from what they say. Find out what other people who know them well think and about how the person has reacted in the past. Their family and close friends may be able to help you. If necessary ask a specialist such as a speech and language therapist to help you.

When you speak, express yourself as clearly as possible. Use short sentences and simple words (without speaking to the person as if they were a child). Make sure you have the person's full attention. It can sometimes help to say their name first, so they know you are talking to them. Remember that many people can take things very literally. Be careful with your use of humour or phrases that can be misleading. We often say things that we don't intend to be taken literally without realising. Think about your tone of voice too – this can often help the person to focus on what you are saying if you make it match your topic.

Use plenty of non-verbal communication (such as facial expressions, eye gaze, gestures, body language) to support your speech. This will help the person to understand even if they cannot understand all your words. It is often very helpful to use other visual communication (written material, photographs, videos, pictures, symbols, objects, etc.). These can explain in another way what you are trying to say. Sometimes showing the person what you mean by demonstrating or going on a visit can be very useful. Remember that if the person is a reactive communicator they will only make sense of things as they experience them. You will need to observe their reactions over a period of time for you to know what they feel about something.

Don't rush. You will need to take more time and if necessary repeat your message on several occasions to check out whether somebody has understood. Simply asking someone to repeat what you have said does not mean they have necessarily understood. Watch carefully for their reactions to give you clues that they may have misunderstood.

There are no easy short-cuts to any of this. If you are trying to explain something particularly important, it is worth taking time to prepare. Try jotting down what you want to say and work out how you plan to explain this to the person beforehand. Get any materials such as drawings or objects ready to take with you. Think about where and when you are going to talk to the person. All this preparation really helps.

Getting support for communication

Translation and interpretation services

People whose preferred language is not the language of the majority community may require the support of a translator or interpreter. This could for example be somebody who uses British Sign Language. It could also be somebody whose

first language is Polish, for example. Translators are people who translate written documents from one language to another language. Interpreters are people who translate spoken or signed words from one language to another. Most areas will have established translation and interpreter services. It is not normally good practice to use other family members to take on this role as it can breach confidentiality and have an impact on family relationships.

> **Thinking point**
>
> *If one of the people you support or their family requires an interpreter or a translator, do you know how you would obtain one for them? If not, how can you find this out?*

Easy-read information

Some people can benefit from written information being put into an easy-read format. This involves the use of simple sentences and language and the use of photos or pictures to support the meaning of the written words.

Advocacy services

> Advocacy is taking action to help people say what they want, secure their rights, represent their interests and obtain services they need. Advocacy promotes social inclusion, equality and social justice.
>
> Advocacy Charter: Action in Advocacy, 2002

Advocacy is an important way for people with learning disabilities to have more choice and control in their lives. Advocacy works in different ways and can take a number of forms but operates on certain basic principles and approaches. People you support could benefit from an advocate to support them to speak up for themselves and make their views known.

Some will have a right to a special kind of advocate (an Independent Mental Capacity Advocate – IMCA) under some circumstances.

> **Thinking point**
>
> *Under what circumstances would you consider involving an advocate for one of the people you support? Do you know where to access this service locally? If not, find out.*

Speech and language therapy

Speech and language therapists can support people with learning disabilities with both their communication and also chewing and swallowing. They are often based in community learning disability teams. They are specialists in communication and can assess the person's communication needs and advise you how best to meet these. You can contact your local speech and language therapy service for advice about any aspect of communication with the people you support.

Sophie and the speech and language therapy referral

Although Sophie is very chatty, her support team leader was worried that she was becoming confused when people were talking to her about important decisions in her life. Sophie agreed it would be a good idea to ask the speech and language therapist for ideas to help. The therapist spent some time with Sophie and chatted to the team. She pointed out to Sophie and her staff the kind of things Sophie found confusing. She suggested ways they could improve communication. The therapist wrote these ideas in a report for Sophie and her support team. She also wrote a simple communication passport which summarised the best ways to communicate with Sophie. This gave the staff lots of ideas, mainly about ways they could change their communication. Every new person who works with Sophie now reads the passport so they can communicate well with Sophie – and Sophie herself knows what her supporters need to remember. She will use the passport to check out people's communication skills when she and her fiancé interview for support workers for their new life together.

Key points from this chapter

- You can't overstate the importance of communication, without it you can't interact, and without interactions you can't have a relationship and without a relationship I don't think one can have a life of any real sort.

(Clinical Psychologist quoted in the Intensive Interaction Newsletter, Issue 18, Winter 2006/7)

- Effective communication is one of the most important skills you need in your job supporting people with a learning disability.

- To communicate effectively with a person with a learning disability, you need to believe in their right to communicate and be communicated with.

- Be patient and give people time to think about what they want to say and time to get their message across.

- You should apply the principles of total communication and use lots of different methods – sign language, symbols and pictures as appropriate.

- Be careful not to assume that because someone doesn't speak they can't understand you, or that because they can speak they'll understand everything you say.

References and where to go for more information

Websites

Action 4 Advocacy www.actionforadvocacy.org.uk

Association of Sign Language www.asli.org.uk

British Institute of Learning Disabilities www.bild.org.uk

Easy Health www.easyhealth.org.uk Easy read health information on a wide range of topics including ears and eyes

Elizabeth Fitzroy Support www.efitzroy.org.uk

Hearing and Learning Disabilities www.hald.org.uk For all concerned about people with learning disabilities and hearing loss

Look Up www.lookupinfo.org About people with learning disabilities and their eye care needs

Register of Public Services Interpreters www.nrpsi.co.uk

Royal College of Speech and Language Therapists www.rcslt.org

SeeAbility www.seeability.org About blind or partially sighted people who have additional disabilities

Chapter 4

Applying principles and practices of confidentiality in your work

> *What do you think confidential means?*

> *Edward: Private and personal*

> *What does 'keeping things confidential' mean?*

> *Sophie: It means other people can't read what's been written down on a piece of paper or if it's very important like in personal folder and then they are not allowed to read anything what's in it. We go upstairs and we talk about it in private bedroom between us and we discuss everything like the doctors and we just keep it ourselves.*

Introduction

When you were appointed to your job, you agreed to maintain principles of confidentiality at all times as part of doing a professional job. This chapter looks at some of the practical issues you face in doing this.

Knowing that somebody else has access to a lot of personal information about you would probably make you feel very exposed. You would want to make sure that you could trust that person. As a support worker you are in a trusted position and have access to very personal and confidential information about individuals and their families. The Human Rights Act (article 8) says that everyone has the right to a private and family life. You can support this by making sure you maintain confidentiality in your work.

Stop for a minute and think just how much you know about the personal lives of the people with learning disabilities you work with. This may include detailed personal history (possibly even details of their birth and childhood), their family background, intimate medical information, assessments of what they can and can't do, and many other aspects of their life. How would you feel if somebody had this much information about you?

Learning outcomes

This chapter will help you to:

- explain the meaning of the term 'confidentiality' in your work role;

- describe the potential tension between maintaining an individual's confidentiality and disclosing concerns;

- demonstrate ways to maintain confidentiality in day-to-day communication;

- explain how, when and from whom to seek advice about confidentiality.

This chapter covers:

- Common Induction Standards – Standard 3 – Communicate effectively: Learning Outcome 4

- Level 2 SHC 21 – Introduction to communication: Learning Outcome 5

- Level 3 SHC 31 – Promote communication: Learning Outcome 4

What do we mean by confidentiality?

Confidentiality must not be confused with secrecy. Confidentiality means respecting personal information about individuals and their families and carers, and keeping this information private. It also means not disclosing this information to others unless an appropriate person, or people, gives you permission to do so. This will usually be the person with a learning disability, unless there are good and acceptable reasons why not. This means that as a support worker you should keep confidential any personal information about the person you support, whilst you are employed to work with them and also afterwards.

It is essential that you should both understand why confidentiality is important in working with people who have learning disabilities, and also be able to explain this to others. This is not always easy. You may find that family and friends and fellow professionals all feel they have an automatic right to information about a person you support.

Thinking point

Is it always right to keep information confidential? Can you think of a situation where it would be important for someone to disclose information about you that should otherwise be kept confidential?

Understanding the limits and boundaries to confidentiality

Working with a person with learning disabilities is based on a relationship of trust. Confidentiality is a daily issue for this relationship. It is wise, so far as possible, to establish limits to confidentiality at the beginning. It may be necessary to involve not only the person with a learning disability, but family, other close carers and line managers.

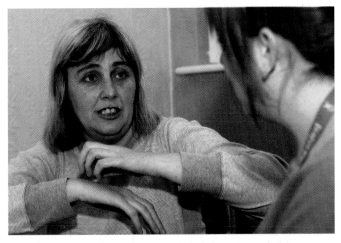

Working with a person with disabilities is based on a relationship of trust.

When the person you support has the capacity to understand the decision to be made about sharing information, you should respect their wishes. Where they lack that capacity, you must follow the principles of relevant capacity legislation in acting in their best interests.

In England and Wales:

Mental Capacity Act (2005)

In Scotland:

Adults with Incapacity (Scotland) Act 2000

In Northern Ireland:

Currently dealt with under common law although there are plans to introduce capacity legislation

In all cases it is important that you are honest with the people you support and explain you may have to break a confidence. Advocacy workers often deal with this by making it clear from their very first contact with the person that they will maintain confidentiality except in certain clear circumstances. This is a useful model to follow.

People who have severe or profound learning disabilities may be particularly vulnerable to situations where confidentiality has to be breached. They may not understand or may find it difficult to communicate about issues of confidentiality. It is still important, however, to maintain the principles and practices of confidentiality so far as possible.

If you are unsure what to do, think about what other care partners, such as family carers, might need to know to be able to give good support. Then ask permission to share the information, explaining why it might be helpful to share. You will need to record how you explained this to the person and their response. Always ask your line manager or a senior colleague if you are unsure, or refer to your organisation's confidentiality policy.

Professional responsibility

The General Social Care Council (GSCC) is the organisation set up by the government in 2001, to register and regulate all social care workers in England. Similar bodies exist in Scotland, Wales and Northern Ireland. Their Codes of Practice outline the standards that all social care workers should keep. You should make sure you get a copy, read it and follow what it says about confidentiality.

The code of practice states that as a social care worker:

- you must strive to establish and maintain the trust and confidence of service users and carers. This includes respecting confidential information and clearly explaining agency policies about confidentiality to service users and carers;
- you must uphold public trust and confidence in social care services. In particular you must not abuse the trust of service users and carers or the access you have to personal information about them or to their property, home or workplace.

By 2012 the functions of the GSCC will be transferred to the Health Professions Council (HPC) which will be given a new title to reflect its new responsibilities. You will need to look out for any material or guidance that is produced by this new organisation.

Can confidentiality ever be breached?

You should assume that in most situations you should never breach confidentiality. But there are times when you may have to do this in the best interests of the person or where there is a duty to protect the wider public interest. For example, if you suspect someone is being abused, you must report it, even if the person who told you about it asks you not to say anything. Always seek guidance from managers or senior colleagues when this situation arises.

Breaching confidentiality

Times will occur in your work when confidentiality needs to be breached. Making a decision on confidentiality can be difficult. Thinking carefully about it, refering to your organisation's policies and discussing with others concerned will help you not only decide, but be ready to defend the decision you make. There are some helpful principles on which you can base your thinking and decisions about breaching confidentiality.

Always think about:

- whether or not the person is competent to decide and has given informed consent to the sharing of the information;
- the balance between the person's right to confidentiality and the danger that will result if you do not disclose information;
- what the confidentiality policy says;
- the balance between risk-taking and the duty of care;
- the degree of risk that someone will come to significant harm;
- the views of family, friends and any advocate;
- the views of your senior managers and experienced colleagues.

You should not normally come to a decision about breaching confidentiality alone. Except in rare cases where an emergency decision has to be reached, it is standard good practice to consult with the person themselves and others concerned.

Activity

Keeping the golden rules. These rules have been drawn from government guidance on information sharing. Take a look at these rules and discuss with your colleagues how they apply in your work.

1. **Remember the Data Protection Act is not a barrier** *to sharing information. It is a framework to make sure personal information is shared appropriately.*
2. **Be open and honest from the start** *with the person (and their family as appropriate) about why, what, how and with whom information could be shared. Seek their agreement, unless it is unsafe or inappropriate to do so.*
3. **Seek advice** *if you are in any doubt, without disclosing the identity of the person where possible.*
4. **Share with consent where appropriate** *and, where possible, respect the wishes of those who do not consent. You may share without consent if, in your judgement, that lack of consent can be overridden in the public interest.*
5. **Consider safety and well-being.** *Base decisions by considering the safety and well-being of the person and others who may be affected by their actions.*
6. **Necessary, proportionate, relevant, accurate, timely and secure.** *Ensure that what you share is necessary for the purpose for which you are sharing it, is shared only with those people who need to have it, is accurate and up to date, is shared in a timely fashion, and is shared securely.*
7. **Keep a record** *of your decision and the reasons for it – whether it is to share information or not. If you decide to share, then record what you have shared, with whom and for what purpose.*

(Adapted from HM Government Information Sharing: Guidance for Practitioners and Managers)

Personal assistants

Self-directed support is a system of social care that puts people in charge of their own support. It means that a person with learning disabilities can employ people, including family members, as part of this support using a direct payment or personal budget to pay people's wages. People managing their own support this way, some with family help, employ their own personal assistants. It is important that the principles of confidentiality are followed here also. Contracts of employment should make clear the need to maintain confidentiality and when it may need to be breached. If you are a personal assistant and have any concerns about confidentiality, you should discuss it with your employer.

> **Thinking point**
>
> *If you were the family carer of a person you support, is there anything particular you would need to be aware of in relation to confidentiality?*

Understanding your organisation's confidentiality policies and procedures

Every organisation should take confidentiality very seriously and have policies and procedures that tell staff what is required of them. This information should also be available to the people who use your service as well as family carers and friends. The Data Protection Act 1998 has guidelines your organisation needs to follow when collecting and storing confidential information.

You may also hear people talk about the Caldicott Principles. These are guidelines that are followed by social care and health professionals when using confidential information in which a person's personal details are included. These principles state that you should:

- justify the purpose of using information that identifies the person concerned;
- only use personally identifiable information when absolutely necessary;
- use the minimum personally identifiable information that is required;
- only allow access to this information on a strict need-to-know basis;
- make sure everyone who has access to the information understands his or her responsibilities;
- understand and comply with the law.

The Data Protection Act 1998 also has eight further principles which must also be followed when dealing with confidential and personal information. You can find more about this in *A Guide to Data Protection* produced by the Information Commissioner's Office (2009).

Your organisation's policies and procedures are likely to include reference to both the Caldicott Principles and the Data Protection Act. If policies and procedures are to work well within your organisation, you should know where to find them and how to use them.

Activity

Here is a checklist for you to check your knowledge of your organisation's policies and procedures on confidentiality. Can you answer the questions confidently?

- *Where are your organisation's policies and procedures on confidentiality normally kept and how do you access them if you need them?*

- *If you were unclear about something written in these documents, who would be the best person to explain it to you?*

- *If the parents or other close relatives of a person you support complained to you about a breach of confidentiality, what would you do about it?*

- *If you felt that a colleague had breached confidentiality, what would you do?*

- *If you had, by mistake, passed on information that was confidential, what would you do and whom would you talk to?*

- *If there was a serious breach of confidentiality in your service, what disciplinary procedures would be taken, and by whom?*

If you cannot readily answer questions of this kind, you should refresh your knowledge of the main points of your organisation's policies and procedures on sharing information with others before you go further with this section. If there are any points on which you are unclear, raise them with your line manager.

Practical ways to support and maintain confidentiality

Good practice in relation to confidentiality in the workplace can involve a number of factors that need to become second nature in the way you work. There are times when it is easy to remember when confidentiality needs to be maintained. This is when something significant, dramatic or unusual occurs. On the other hand, it is when dealing with routine that we may slip up and breach confidentiality. Trust is crucial to your relationship with the person you support. If it is lost over a breach of confidentiality with even a small matter, this can cause strong emotional reactions, and it may be a long time before the damage is repaired.

Confidentiality in day-to-day working

Your everyday work will often mean you receive confidential information in a number of ways. There are some practical steps you can take to maintain confidentiality in the way you handle this information.

As a support worker you are in a trusted position and have access to very personal and confidential information about individuals and their families.

It is important that you:

- respect confidences;
- always assume that something personal is confidential unless the person concerned tells you otherwise;
- help the people you support to understand what you can and cannot keep confidential;
- do not make promises you cannot keep about keeping everything private;
- discourage the people you support from giving you unnecessary personal or private information;
- use the most private way to pass on private and personal information.

When confidential information is written you should:

- put confidential papers away safely after using them;
- only use faxes or emails that are password-protected;
- anonymise any written material that is shared, for example in a training situation;
- make sure you don't leave information on a computer screen open for all to see.

When you talk to anyone about confidential information you should:

- have private conversations, both face-to-face and by telephone, in places where you cannot be overheard;

- not refer to matters that are personal to a particular person in groups, whether staff or people who use your service;

- guide people you work with away from talking about private, family or personal matters in public;

- not report to relatives anything that a person with learning disabilities may have told you about private family matters;

- be careful about how you phrase confidential information when you have to pass it on to someone else;

- not discuss confidential information with colleagues, assuming that they also know about it.

Access to confidential information

An important aspect of confidentiality is checking people's identity before they have access to information. There are issues of security and of health and safety involved also. Your policies and procedures should give guidance on this, and you should be familiar with these.

There are several reasons why this is important. These include:

- passing on information without authorisation is against the rights of an individual;

- disclosing information can result in intrusion into an individual's private affairs;

- it shows lack of respect for the privacy and individuality of the person you support and their family;

- there are legal requirements relating to keeping information confidential;

- information should be passed on only to other people with the right to have access to it;

- sharing information unwisely or unnecessarily will reflect badly not only on the person who discloses the information, but also on the service.

Consider the following before allowing access to confidential information.

- Assume all personal information is confidential unless you know otherwise.

- Unless you have clear authority to do so, never disclose information about people without checking with your line manager.

- In general, never disclose possibly confidential information about people over the telephone.

Never disclose private or personal information about a person by phone or in a meeting unless given permission to do so.

- If telephoned information is required urgently, e.g. by the person's GP or a hospital, check with senior staff if possible and then call the enquirer back on a number that you can check first.

- Never disclose private or personal information about a person in a meeting on or off the premises unless given permission to do so by the person, if they are able to do this, and your line manager.

Access to people's homes

If you are a support worker who works with people with learning disabilities in their family home, or their own home, you will need to follow the access arrangements agreed in the person's support plan. You must always remember that it is the person's home you are working in and generally you should ring the bell and wait to be invited in. You should hold a key to the person's home only if there is good reason and it is clearly laid out in their support plan. If you hold a key to the person's home, you should always follow the key-holding policy of your organisation in order that the keys are kept as safe as possible at all times. You should always knock before entering even if you have a key and the person is unable to answer the door.

The person whose home you are working in always has the right to say who they will have in their home and you should respect that right. As someone working in the person's home you should always act honestly and respect their home and property.

You should:

- never enter their home when they are not there (unless by earlier agreement);
- follow your organisation's policy on gifts and borrowing possessions;
- never use any equipment such as phones, CDs, radios or kettles without permission.

Access to your organisation's premises

You should also consider issues of confidentiality before allowing people access to a home, day centre or other property run by the organisation you work for.

Always consider the following.

- Always check the identity of anyone seeking entry to the premises.
- Ask to see ID with a photograph – most professionals are trained to offer this from the start, including people from utilities companies, local authorities, etc.
- Don't allow visitors to wander around unaccompanied unless you have checked that they have the authority to do so.
- If you find someone wandering around, ask if you can help and accompany the person to the office.
- If you see anyone acting suspiciously, call the manager or a senior member of staff.
- If in doubt, make a telephone check to the visitor's organisation, or call the police.

Key points from this chapter

- Confidentiality is an important part of being a learning disability worker.
- Your organisation's policies and procedures will help you to know what to do if you need to breach confidentiality for any reason.
- Always pass on confidential information in the most private way possible.
- Before you breach confidentiality requirements check with the policy and a senior colleague.

References and where to go for more information

References

British Institute of Human Rights (2008) *Your Human Rights – A Guide for Disabled People.* London: BIHR

Department for Constitutional Affairs (2006) *A Guide to the Human Rights Act 1998, third edition.* London: TSO

Department for Constitutional Affairs (2007) *Mental Capacity Act (2005) Code of Practice.* London: TSO

Finnegan, P and Clarke, S (2005) *One Law for All? The impact of the Human Rights Act on People with Learning Disabilities.* London: VIA

Hardie, E and Brooks, L (2009) *Brief Guide to the Mental Capacity Act 2005.* Kidderminster: BILD

HM Government (2008) *Information Sharing: Guidance for practitioners and managers* www.education.gov.uk

Hughes, A and Coombs, P (2001) *Easy Guide to the Human Rights Act 1998.* Kidderminster: BILD

Information Commissioner's office (2009) *A Guide to Data Protection* www.ico.gov.uk accessed 10/8/10

The Scottish Government (2008) *Adults with Incapacity (Scotland) Act 2000: A short guide to the Act* www.scotland.gov.uk

Websites

Information Commissioner's Office www.ico.gov.uk Details of the offices in England, Wales, Scotland and Northern Ireland can be accessed here

The Social Care Councils (responsible for the *Codes of Practice for Social Care Workers*):

Care Council for Wales www.ccwales.org.uk
General Social Care Council (England) www.gscc.org.uk
Northern Ireland Social Care Council www.niscc.info
Scottish Social Services Council www.sssc.uk.com

Social Care Institute for Excellence www.scie.org.uk

Glossary

Communication – the way that two or more people make contact, build relationships and share messages. These messages can be ideas, thoughts or feelings as well as information and questions. Communication involves both sending and understanding these messages and can be done through many different ways including speech, writing, drawing, pictures, symbols, signs, pointing and body language for example.

Communication aids – can range from simple boards or books to more sophisticated devices. They can use pictures or words or symbols. 'Voice output communication aids' are those that can be operated by eye gaze, switches, keyboards or touch screens to trigger spoken messages. A **Lightwriter®** is an example of a voice output communication aid where the user types a message onto a keyboard.

Non-verbal communication – communication that does not use words but uses gesture, body language, signing, symbols, objects of reference and other communication aids.

Objects of reference – a way to communicate using objects to represent words and ideas. Objects of reference are often used for people who cannot either see or understand pictures. For example, showing a person a mug to ask whether they want a drink of tea.

Signs – hand gestures that are used in an agreed way to communicate. Signs from British Sign Language (BSL) have been used in several vocabularies specifically for people with learning disabilities such as Makaton and Signalong.

Symbols – line drawings that are used in an agreed way to communicate. There are many different symbols systems designed for use with people with learning disabilities including Widget, Rebus and Makaton. There are black and white and coloured symbols.

Verbal communication – communication that uses words (either spoken or written).

Index

Added to a page number 'g' denotes glossary.